The Bed Book

Kimberly L. Becker

SPUYTEN DUYVIL
New York City

© 2020 Kimberly L. Becker
ISBN 978-1-952419-34-8
Cover Art: *The Dream (The Bed)*, 1940, Frida Kahlo

Library of Congress Cataloging-in-Publication Data

Names: Becker, Kimberly L., author.
Title: The bed book / Kimberly L. Becker.
Description: New York City : Spuyten Duyvil, [2020] |
Identifiers: LCCN 2020044696 | ISBN 9781952419348 (paperback)
Subjects: LCGFT: Poetry.
Classification: LCC PS3602.E2896 B43 2020 | DDC 811/.6--dc23
LC record available at https://lccn.loc.gov/2020044696

For my son, Alex,
and in loving memory of our spirit dog, Anna,
who guards even now

With deep respect and gratitude to Laurie A. Scudder,
4th Fighter Wing, Sexual Assault Response Coordinator,
warrior for justice and truth

To all survivors of historical,
intergenerational,
or personal trauma

...Most Beds are Beds
for sleeping or resting,
but the best Beds are much
more interesting!

...Not just a white little
tucked-in-tight little
nighty-night little
turn-out-the-light little
bed!
—Sylvia Plath, *The Bed Book*

Parts

HEAD

Creek Bed	3
Ghost Room Bed	4
Make-Believe Bed	5
Backseat Bed	6
Dollhouse Bed	7
Alarm Bed	8
The Little Bed	9
The Flying Bed	10
Bed in the Jungle	11
The Bed and the Mirror	12
Q & A Bed	13
Beer Room Bed	14
Stepping from Bed to Bed	15
The Bed at Hitler's Rasthaus	16

LEGS

Fire Bed	19
Recovery Bed	20
Under the Bed	21
Honey Bed	22
A Bed to Lie In	23
Ice Bed	24
First Bed	25
The Just-Right Bed	26
The Unmade Bed	27
River Bed	28
Bed of Imagined Rest	29
Snug Bed	30
Center Bed	31
Warning Bed	32

FRAME

Foxes' Bed	35
Feather Bed	36
Airport Bed	37
Bed Framed	38
Bed Bug	39
Pop-Up Bed	40
The Beds of Children	41
Deathbed	42
Sleigh Bed	43
Red Letter Bed	44
Sorrow Bed	45
Bed of Intensive Care	46
Royal Bed	47
Judgment Bed	48

FOOT

Bed of Visitation	51
Hammock Bed	52
The Unused Bed	53
Snow Bed	54
Beside the Bed	55
The Bed of Your Skin	56
Non-Dominant Bed	57
Bed of Perfect Detachment	58
Water Bed	59
Monastery Bed	60
Helium Bed	61
Bed Never Lain In	62
Apocalypse Bed	63
Bed of Transformation	64
The Bed in This Cabin	65

HEAD

CREEK BED

My mother
remembers the colors
on the wall the day
she was born
Years later I would
sleep in her childhood room,
in her parents' bed,
and hear screech owls
whinnying at night
(that my grandmother
said meant death)
I'd lie very still
and try not to breathe
until the feathered angel
of death passed by
Years after that,
my dog would jump up
and turn and find her place
We'd both lie there in the dark
She would sleep while the wind
knocked the old metal blinds
against the sill and the creek
made suggestions in the distance

Ghost Room Bed

The bed was heavy
and carved and dark
The white chamber pot
under the bed
the only witness
when the ghost came
and pressed the girl
down to the bed
so she couldn't breathe or move
The girl waited for it to be over,
waited for the ghost to leave
She never breathed a word
to anyone, never breathed
again, not really, not freely,
never relieved herself
of the many-chambered story
The ghost room bed
was heavy and carved and dark
The chamber pot
under the bed
still holds the never-emptied waste
Its overfill still spills and smells
and goes unremarked

Make-Believe Bed

Waking up happy,
if alone,
in luxe hotel bed,
taking a photograph
for you of my smiling face
ring hand on chest,
diamond winking its lies
You make your bed,
you lie in it
Housekeeping came
and swept it all away—
remaking the bed
that was long made

Backseat Bed

Beds don't have to be beds
They can be
padded seat,
burgundy velour,
of land yacht coupe
(Tootsie Pops to mask the taste)
or sandstrewn seat
of finned sedan
You still get carsick
in the back

Dollhouse Bed

Bed your great somebody made,
now holds your child
Pushing play
on cassette for stories
and music to sleep by
Sometimes cats
come and curl up
Across the room,
the bed in the room
of the dollhouse
your grandfather made—
that bed never moves
although years ago
another cat
had slept in that
same dollhouse,
dislodging
miniature furniture
As adults are always entering
the world of children,
forcing themselves
to fit where they shouldn't
ever even be

Alarm Bed

You fall asleep
to treasured words,
You know you're special,
don't you? You're my girl
But ghosts patrol
outside and press
against the glass
and press within
from dreams
so that you wet the bed
(no chamber pot and
bathroom too far to go in terror)
Such a bad thing
for such a big girl
Special padding
on the mattress sets off alarm
that sounds years earlier
in the ghost room,
in the beer room
Grownups came running
and shaming
oblivious to other alarms
they always failed to hear

The Little Bed

What we called
the little bed
came apart to slats,
carved head
and footboards,
legs with frame
(as if a bed
had body parts)
Custom narrow mattress
slid down inside,
body into shallow grave
Daybed, nightbed
depending on that
generation's use
Your son graduated
to little bed from crib
by window
with blue drapes
and shadows of *Birds!*
You put a guard rail
on the little bed
as if your son would drive
too fast in sleep
There were
no guardrails on your beds
no guards within, without

The Flying Bed

In the movie
there was a flying bed
There was a witch
and a mountain
and it was easy
to imagine
my own bed
flying over the mountain
away from the witch
or whatever was bad
The way my body
would fly away
and wait on the ceiling
The way you started
watching your life
like watching a movie,
from a safe distance

BED IN THE JUNGLE

The bed in the jungle
had greenleaved canopy
Low growl of large animal
you couldn't see
since your head
was down
but later knew
must have come from him
You pretended you were on safari
He told you he'd been to a real jungle
and that camouflage was important:
never tell, never be seen
It was your secret game
Sun on the leaves, leaves
in your hair, his paws on your head,
and when his low growl stopped
You would metamorphose
back into a girl as he removed
traces of leaves and branches
from your hair and clothes,
promising Pepsi,
promising ice cream,
promising piggybank lion
you'd seen and coveted,
chips of sapphire for eyes
that you thought were real
Meanwhile, your imaginary lion
follows you from the jungle
as dense green closes behind
leaving no sign
of maneuvers

The Bed and the Mirror

The bed with the mirror
above it on the ceiling
meant it was hard
for her to fly away
without flying into glass
like red cardinal found
with broken neck
from seeking its reflection
in the window
blood at the beak
no song to speak

Q & A Bed

Look at him
curled in the little bed
turned away in pain
You did this
He turns to
face you now
mouths *why?*
You have so
many answers
so many beds
with their knowing
heads,
nodding

Beer Room Bed

The bed in the beer room
was a twin, as if beds
are related and lonely
when separated
Your father had a twin
or maybe older brother
you never can remember
But you remember
your grandfather's
thrilling terrifying telling
of seeing the ghost
of the dead brother
or vision of brother
who was about to die
Stories stay with you
The twin bed in the beer room
had a ribbed bedspread
you remember the feel of
just as later you'll remember
feel of burgundy velour
in the back of a car
You are always sleepy
in the beer room
everything always blurry
Because first you always
have *root beer*, foamy and frothy
making things fuzzy and hazy
and goldy sunshiny
so dozy you never miss your clothesies

Stepping from Bed to Bed

Stepping from bed to bed
like stepping stones,
I step again onto your bed
where your husband
and his mistress lay beside you
as you were working at dying
Stern angel watched at the head
of the bed while we planned
your celebration
I promised yes to every wish
When you finally flew away,
you were all iridescence, freed

The Bed at Hitler's Rasthaus

Red wine spills like blood
black-out curtains
black out
Let's agree
there are degrees
of atrocities
No one had a choice
At breakfast
people look away
No one says a word,
complicit in silence
At night,
the statue of the mermaid
steps free from her pedestal,
dives into the lake
Ripples widen then cease
She brings bodies to the surface,
tells them stories to revive them

LEGS

Fire Bed

You may be getting tired
of beds by now
Look—there is a bed
already turned down
Let's tuck you in,
up to your chin
Never fear:
the fire isn't real
Always fear:
of course the fire is real
You yell *Fire!* anyway
But you're in a silent movie
Your voice goes unheard
as flames rise to cover screams
you never can turn down

Recovery Bed

Pain and nausea
Nurse asks to switch
from morphine to dilaudid
How you love the soothing
names of soothing drugs,
like characters
in children's books
Nurse helps you
to the toilet, your
non-slip socks
coded red for risk
Surgeon speaks from
foot of the bed
detailing what he did
to your brain while you
slept
Now you sleep between
vitals checks
Packet of crackers,
cup of ginger ale
small blessings on tray table
This is a safe bed
But you keep the call button close

Under the Bed

She'd have to go
get her own switch
and present it to him
He would cut the air
to test its worth
as she ran to hide
He would chase her,
but was no match
against the quickness of her youth
She'd shimmy under the bed
in the back room
You know the room—
the one with the guns on the wall
and the little white hard-sided
suitcase under the bed
next to gold-striped hat boxes
The bedspread was white chenille
Its raised design felt like it told a story
It hung down low
and she would peer through
tassels of fringe
as his work boots came into view
He knew she was there
and would swipe under the bed
but couldn't reach to pull her out
She'd swat back at him
No she didn't. She knew better.
But she wanted to.
He'd get tired and switch off the light.
She'd wait until it was safe
before she came out
She never came out

Honey Bed

Beach where shark came close
as new husband swam alone
At night someone
rattled the knob
of the door to your room
pleading, *Honey?*
Are you in there, honey?
Then threatening,
I will deal with you,
don't think I won't
As they packed to go
she made the bed
and made it promise
not to tell

A Bed to Lie In

Pink shag carpet
Ponies and Barbies
He asked you
pointed
question
Your words and body lied
to hide
your real reply

Ice Bed

The bed
of games
of almost-but-not-quite
We had to be quiet
All the other beds
hung like dirigibles
advertising loss
You floated up,
stepping mattress to mattress
sinking into different memories
While below, his face
was coming closer for a kiss,
distorted, as if from under ice
In the freezer,
ice cubes settled
in their beds of trays

First Bed

Full fathom five your father lies
Basement apartment
Shakespeare to impress/undress
But the bed was crowded with ghosts
and memory rose to flood level
At first the bed floated,
awkwardly knocking
into other furniture
Then it went under,
covered
Those are pearls that were his eyes

The Just-Right Bed

But, you say,
there had to have been
a bed just right
not too hard,
not too soft

Let me think

Yes, there was one
that came pretty close
where we built a tent
of quilts and looked through
to light like stained glass
and where I didn't float away
but stayed

There was that one bed
that one time,
but you never went back

The Unmade Bed

The bed at your place
was never made
We started to go
through the motions
but realized we were both
on the ceiling, so we lay
and told stories instead
How your incested sister died
in bed, choking on gum
How each of us,
separately, as children,
pretended the ceiling
was the floor and how
we'd crouch in angles
created by walls and rooves
We finally stopped talking
and lay untouching,
relieved of pretending
that we were otherwise made

River Bed

In the bed by the river
they each played a role:
what do you want me to be
her body asked his
mine and malleable
his tacit reply
She watched from above
as he arranged her limbs
to his liking
The river knew nothing
of faithlessness,
but the bed had seen it all
so that when they left,
it threw its covers off
and laughed til its legs
shook the floor
while river flowed over lasting bed

Bed of Imagined Rest

She imagines
a bed where
she will finally rest
and wake to sunlight slatted
through blinds
in bars of incarceration
Instead, she wakes
in dread sweat
in the dark
Wills her heart
to stop pounding
so loud to get out,
wills her breath to stop picking
the lock of her lungs,
lest the ghost will hear
and come at her again

Snug Bed

This bed
is very
snug.
The pillow
is just right.
The covers
not too tight.
No need
for a nightlight.
You sleep
but dream
of blood.

Center Bed

The bed at the center
of the house
was less used
It was the back-up bed
on childhood map
not drawn to scale
That bed is blank as a starter's gun
Whatever happened here,
she wasn't there
Whatever happened there,
she isn't here
She sees her hair spread
on white sheets white pillow
Hears the roaches'
dim scurries as door opens
softly
The bed at the center
of the house was closest
to the garage outside
where she saw crushed kitten's skull
Walk around to the right
to side yard where palmetto
cut her hands
when she held it tight
in mock weaponry
but froze in fear at night
without defense

Warning Bed

I should have put this   *from the ceiling
at the beginning,
but here is your warning
laid out in rose-red letters
on spread of waiting bed:

These bedtime stories
are not suitable for children
and could possibly be disturbing
for underage readers
*or adults who watch

FRAME

FRAME

Foxes' Bed

Mythical cartography
that never changes:
set in rock
in mountainside,
the foxes' den
You would slip in
after them,
their pointed faces
spoke welcome
as their tails twitched fire
Before leaving for the night,
they'd tuck you in
You'd listen as they
screamed for mates
between their hunts
You preferred the den to bed
In den you were safe,
part of their earth
In bed you were prey,
your own screams mute

Feather Bed

In feather bed
(don't think of source)
under feather covers
(more animal use for comfort)
they covered
each other with kisses
Ornate furniture barely
discernible in dark of the room
In the cold,
mingled breath was visible
when they came up for air
They had to keep quiet
so she found a scrap of paper
and scribbled note with pen
whose ink she had to shake awake:
Do what you want
but he already had

Airport Bed

The beds in airport hotels,
one time shared with stranger
to avoid sleeping in terminal
Another time alone
after coast-to-coast flight
and refusal of offered company
Those beds were like
suitcases you packed
yourself into temporarily
then circled the carousel of dreams

Bed Framed

I kept trying
to tell them
what happened
but they listened
to the bed instead
that only saw the surface
of what happened,
not all the red
soaked through
to mattress pad
to mattress
The frame was intact
The frame is whom
they believed
not me on top
of it
with you
on top
of me
The floor was just
as floored
thinking back on all
it hadn't seen

Bed Bug

The bed bug does
not apologize
for feasting
on slough
of skin
after enough
love has been
simulated
It laughs
when we invoke
its name
in childish
bedtime rhyme,
our skin raised
with telling rash
on our rash untelling skin

Pop-Up Bed

If this were a children's book
there would be
a pop-up bed
and in the bed
a girl and a wolf
(you know the story)
Close the book
the bed retracts
Open the book
it pops back up
Close the book
Open the book
Close the book
Leave it closed
until you hear growls
and muffled screams
Open the book—
no bed
just red

The Beds of Children

Bunk beds
at Terezin
and still children
wrote poems
and drew pictures
of butterflies
In beds
at government
boarding schools,
children cried
themselves
to sleep with tears
in their own language
while black-robed ghosts
came at night
and stole innocence
but never survivance
Children of war
who have no beds
but earth,
bodies used for pleasure
by soldiers
The child's bed
is always fraught
with danger

Deathbed

Hospital bed
brought into the home
Overbed tray
for Chapstick
and chargers, now disused
Cups from pudding
and applesauce
cleared away
when only morphine
was needed
As he slept,
I sat with my hand
on his chest
his breathing labored
until eased with dose
Roles reversed
as if he were the child
Worn-thin white of t-shirt
damp with fever
I tried to say
forgiving things
Meanwhile death
mocked my efforts,
stole the pillow
hogged the covers,
sucked the air
out of the room
with all his pompous stories

Sleigh Bed

Moon pushes light into bedroom
while Mars, startlingly red and large,
barely contained by window frame,
watches me restless,
missing my old dog,
missing what never was
The sleigh bed in our first house—
how the child in me imagined it to be
a real sleigh to carry us away
from all that was *bro-
ken and couldn't be fixed*
That bed had memory foam
that absorbed our dreams
that played on endless loop
Tonight, sans sleigh,
I put away the load of memories
bid goodnight to moon and Mars,
go back to current bed
where my ghost of a dog
circles in celestial light
to find embodied sleep
Growls still emanate from closet
in our first apartment
I dream of sled dogs in Alaska,
fur red in firelight

Red Letter Bed

That time she was dying
and the doctors
couldn't figure out
what was wrong
and from the fire
of fever she called
for her helpmeet
and was told
he had left—
that was when
hospital bed rose
into sterile air
over whitecoats' talking heads,
cleared automatic doors
to lift into violent night,
where it came to hover
over red letter H
on helipad
Help close, but far away

Sorrow Bed

The bed you made
of sorrow,
circling like a dog
to find your place,
turning until it was
tamped down
just right—
instinct of dogs
who used to sleep
in grass
like wolves—
The bed you made
of sorrow,
circling before
settling,
that is the most
comfortable bed
It fits you
it becomes you
and you've become
that bed,
frame to frame

Bed of Intensive Care

Entwined with tubes,
your father lay,
shivering, fevering,
explaining he had
a daughter who lived
where you lived
You insisted that was you
until some old bond pierced
confusion's fog
and lucidly near death
he said the things
he should have said in life
But the bed knew
what the blood had told it:
that sepsis was spreading
And the bed knew what
the lungs had told it:
that fluid was filling
He lay in the bed
poisoned and drowning,
dying, but freeing
The last time you saw him,
the first time you saw him

Royal Bed

He doesn't tuck her in
Doesn't kiss her goodnight
Like a king,
he leans the crown
of his head
down
to be kissed
as he makes kissing sounds
It is their nightly ritual
For years she lives
and sleeps in exile
building her own kingdom
from words
All she has for company
are imaginary animals
and people risen from graves
or from pages of books
All framed by the fire,
burnished, but unburned

JUDGMENT BED

The bed in the room on the left
was where you waited
in dread for the dead
to crash through window frames
at night, splintered wood, broken glass
They will rise from their graves
on Judgment Day
he intoned, as you lay
still as a stone
You slept on a pillow
of fear
and woke
in winding sheet

FOOT

FOOT

Bed of Visitation

After I die
I visit her,
stand at the foot
of her bed
She wakes up
but isn't scared
Why should she be?
She knows me,
although she won't
know for years that
my death was suicide
I stand without
saying anything,
just so she will know
I am okay
Years earlier
I had lifted her up
into leaves of flaming maple
veins shot through with sun
In all my funeral pictures
she is smiling,
acknowledging the light

Hammock Bed

The gauzy beds of the worms
slung between trees
where moths grow and sleep
remind you of the hammock
you slept in then fell from
wind knocked
out of you
as you looked up through
green to blue
Ghost room:
breath forced
from lungs
you tried to fly away
but couldn't move
and never breathed
a word to anyone
Mute worms stir,
beginning to form wings
Soon they will emerge on moth feet
and speak through practical flight

The Unused Bed

There was that time
you were supposed to meet
and stay overnight
at your godmother's house
but that bed went unused
Later you learn there were *anomalies*
in the grades of your teacher
That last night in Germany
you did not go home to bed
but slept in bed of straw
where low sounds of animals
soothed you to sleep
No ghost, no flying away
up to the rafters of the barn
You woke to strong kind arms
with gold in your hair,
remembering the woman
who jumped from the loft
and was instantly paralyzed,
just as you were paralyzed
with fear in other beds, used

Snow Bed

In Fairbanks in December
the room was stifling hot
You kept kicking
the covers down
to the foot of the bed,
but you felt triumphant
to have come this far
alone to this unhistoried bed
The muffled outside light
finally drew you
out of bed
and to the window
where snow glowed
in dim daylight,
unmaking the bed
of your mind
and crumpling time
like kicked-off sheets
Alone beds are always safest
Later, in Bettles,
sled dogs
slept in beds
of snow,
covered by sheets
of changing lights

Beside the Bed

Easy to blame
it on fever
but the being
made of light
sat by her bed
brushed her arm
with limb of white
so that she would know
she would survive
Easy to blame
it on imagination
Easy to dismiss
vision born of desperation
But maybe you know what that's like?
Maybe you've been in that bed?

The Bed of Your Skin

You've never been
at home
in the bed
of your skin,
alien kin

Non-Dominant Bed

Scared
not breathing
hurts
stop
Shh, I'll tell you a story

Bed of Perfect Detachment

They start the IV
and dim the lights
After awhile you lift away
from your body
and begin to fly high and fast,
higher even than the ceiling
You visit other worlds,
whose light has not yet reached us
Prism turns, casting triangles of color
until suddenly everything opens
onto octagon of White Atrium—
pure white detachment:
no pain no judgment
no past just present
No warmth, but better:
freedom from illusion,
knowledge of connection
leading to a quiet delight:
I'm in all the snowflakes and in all the snow
You are in minutiae
You are part of grandeur
No longer confined to body,
you become snow angel
you made in Alaska,
not the freezing
indentation
in soft bedding,
but what was made
by that impression,
a new Being lifting, soaring
through magnetic color of aurora

Water Bed

Bed of bath
covers of warm water
ghost of old dog
comes to stand
beside the tub
as she did in life
You hold out your
finger, touch her nose
You sink into
the watery mattress
and remember water bed
your sister had,
how cat's errant claw
deflated it all
Bath water turns red
Anyone could have
seen this coming
You shake the image
from your head
Flip the drain
Step out into
open towel
as wide as any winding sheet

Monastery Bed

The narrow
monastery bed
is meant
to hold prayer
not bodily desire
It is tucked
into corner
of small cell
Single window
opens onto ancient
high-walled courtyard
with locked gate
One night,
the ghost of a girl
knocks on your door
You stand staring
down the long hall
for a long while
deciding not to follow

Helium Bed

The high, high bed
Tippety top
Just breathe
until breath stops

Bed Never Lain In

How many nights
dreaming of you
dreaming of me
our beds were words,
and every word a grave
You lay down beside me
I looked into your closed eyes
Your child cried
and jarred us awake
I never got to say I loved you
I got to love I never said you
Now I sleep me down to lay you

Apocalypse Bed

> Apocalypse (ἀποκάλυψις) is a Greek word meaning revelation, "an unveiling or unfolding of things not previously known and which could not be known apart from the unveiling"

No peeping Tom, he wanted to be seen,
even if in camouflage of lurid light.
Woken from sleep then paralyzed by fright
at leering purple-face of ghost or demon
peering through open sash, just beyond screen—
heavy heat insect dirge of summer night—
she, slight prey pinned in weak arc of nightlight.
Light as a feather, stiff as a board she seemed.
Decades later flash of revelation—no ghost,
just trick of blue lens in Vietnam-issue
flashlight shone on known molester's face. Most
nights she tongues this bitter berry, juice
purpling teeth gritted over years lost
to fear. Now she spits it out and starts anew.

BED OF TRANSFORMATION

You wake from dream of death
to call of great horned owl
right outside your window
Door slams inside closed room
Who is there with you?
In dark room in dark bed
in dark of night you see
with bright clarity
how you must
die to former self
You lie awake and listen
in ecstatic fear
to owl's calling
owl's warning
owl's truthing

The Bed in This Cabin

On the way to visit
their dying father
they stopped
at their sister's
and slept
on her air mattress
and the bed lifted
and floated through years
and came down
in this cabin
where barred owl
sings death
at night
and they remember
all the beds
and put it all to bed
on the fresh sheets
of this book

Acknowledgments

Thank you to the editors of the following journals for publishing individual poems:

"Hammock Bed," IDK Magazine
"The Beds of Children," North Dakota Quarterly
"Sorrow Bed," Panoply
"Judgment Bed," K'in
"Recovery Bed," Medical Literary Messenger
"Creek Bed," "Ghost Room Bed," "Ice Bed," Vitamin ZZZ
"The Unmade Bed," Storm Cellar
"Bed of Transformation," "Beer Room Bed," "Beside the Bed," "The Flying Bed," "Snow Bed," Two Hawks Quarterly

With appreciation to:

Spuyten Duyvil, especially Aurelia Lavallee, for welcoming my work, for midwifing that last, hard
poem, and for a stunning cover

Wildacres for a residency at Azalea Cabin, where the first draft of this book was written

All my Native sister writers, whose words and witness inform my own life and work

Ann, LCMHC, Dr. Eduardo Duran, Dr. K., Marilyn Weiner, M.S., L.M.F.T., L.C.P.C. Healers, all

In addition to *The Bed Book*, Kimberly L. Becker is author of three other poetry collections: *Words Facing East* and *The Dividings* (WordTech Editions), and *Flight* (forthcoming, MadHat Press). Individual poems appear widely in journals and anthologies, including *Indigenous Message on Water*; *Women Write Resistance: Poets Resist Gender Violence*; and *Tending the Fire: Native Voices and Portraits*. She has held grants from Maryland, North Carolina, and New Jersey and residencies at Hambidge, Weymouth, and Wildacres. Reading venues include Busboys and Poets and The National Museum of the American Indian, Washington, DC. She has served as mentor for PEN America's Prison Writing and AWP's Writer to Writer programs. www.kimberlylbecker.com